Designed by Mary Morioka
and Paula Newcomb

94   5 4 3

Library of Congress Catalog Card Number 88–38669
ISBN 0-8248-1180-1

SAND TO SEA
Marine Life of Hawaii

Stephanie Feeney
Ann Fielding

with photographs by Ed Robinson
and others

A Kolowalu Book • University of Hawaii Press • Honolulu

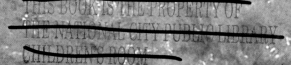

About the Book

The beautiful photographs in this book show the plants and animals that live at the beach, in the tidepools, on the reef, and in the ocean surrounding Hawaii. In the text we describe how the creatures of the sea live, how they protect themselves, and how they interact with each other. We also give guidelines that will help you have a safe and enjoyable experience at the beach and in the water.

This book is written for children, though adults who love the ocean will enjoy it too. We hope that it will help you to know and to appreciate the very special world of Hawaii's shores and ocean.

Let's go to the beach! It's fun to play in the water and dig in the sand. The beach is a good place to begin to learn about marine life—plants and animals that live in the ocean.

photos on pages 1, 6, and 7 by Doug Faulkner

Most beaches in Hawaii have beautiful white sand but some have black sand. Waves pounding for many years grind white coral, black lava rock, and colorful shells into sand. Look carefully at a handful of sand and see if you can tell what it is made of.

On the beach you may find seashells, glass balls, strange-shaped rocks, and pieces of coral and glass washed smooth by the waves.

Sit quietly and watch the sand. You may see small ghost crabs peeping out of their holes or scurrying across the beach.

If you explore the rocky areas near the beach you may see quick, long-legged black crabs (called *a'ama* in Hawaiian) that live on the wave-splashed rocks. They have a hard outer skeleton for protection.

Small sea snails called nerites (also called by their Hawaiian name *pipipi*) and periwinkles live in clusters on the rocks near the ocean. The *pipipi*s are round and black and the periwinkles are grey and pointed.

At high tide the sea covers the rocks near the shore.
At low tide the sea moves away from the shore and some
water is left behind in shallow reef areas and in rocky
tidepools.

When you walk from the shore into the water there is a
whole new world to explore.

During low tide you can see many interesting sights in the
reefs and pools.

Colorful seaweeds live in the shallow water. They get energy from the sun to live and grow. Seaweed provides food, hiding places, and oxygen for sea animals.

Some seaweeds are soft and flexible.

Others are brightly colored and form a hard crust on the rocks.

Doug Faulkner

If you turn over a rock or look in a hole, you may find small crabs, sea urchins, and other animals hiding there.

Colin Lau

Sea urchins are covered with spines that protect them. They have tube feet, which are slender tentacles with suction cups that hold onto the rocks. Rock-boring urchins dig holes in the rocks. Collector urchins hold bits of rock, shell, and seaweed on their bodies.

Sausage-shaped sea cucumbers live on the sand or under rocks. Some of them will squirt out water or sticky white strings if you pick them up.

Black brittle stars live in dark spaces under the rocks. They move very quickly when they are disturbed. A brittle star can break off an arm to escape from predators and grow a new one later.

Soft-bodied snails called sea hares have two pairs of tentacles that look like ears. They live under rocks and around seaweeds.

Colin Lau

Sea snails move by inching their way along on a strong muscle called a foot. The empty shells that you find on the beach were the outer skeletons of sea snails. Sometimes hermit crabs find snail shells and live in them.

Spaghetti worms protect their soft bodies by burrowing between the rocks. They collect food with long white tentacles.

Some fishes live in the safety of tidepools when they are very young; when they get bigger they go to the deeper ocean. Other fishes, including blennies and gobies, live in the tidepools their entire life.

Blennies rest with their tails curled and jump from pool to pool when they are startled.

Gobies (*o'opu* in Hawaiian) dart straight ahead and have a suction cup on their undersides to hold them on the rocks.

In the deeper water beyond the tidepools there are hills
and valleys of rock and coral. This beautiful undersea
world can be explored by snorkeling.

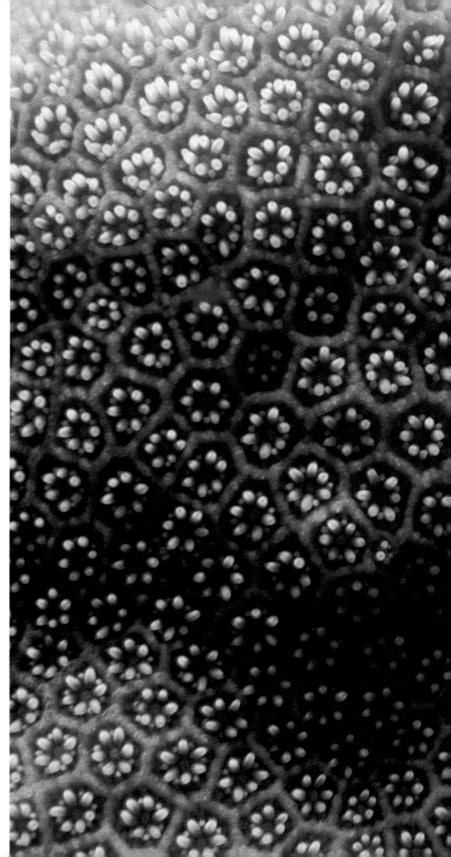

Corals are colonies of tiny flower-shaped animals that secrete hard, white limestone. A coral colony consists of a thin, delicate layer of live animals growing over thick layers of limestone that were produced over many years. The live coral colonies are usually brown or yellow-green, but sometimes they are pink or lavender.

You may see cauliflower-, finger-, and lobe-shaped coral colonies.

Coral reefs are made up of coral colonies, hard seaweeds, and other stoney materials. It takes a long, long time for them to form. Many kinds of sea animals make their homes on and inside the coral reef.

The freckled seastar and the green seastar have five arms. Sometimes a seastar detaches one of its arms and grows a new one. The arm that comes off, called a comet, becomes a new seastar.

The colorful slate-pencil sea urchin wedges between rocks with its spines. If you pick one up and look underneath you can see the mouth has five tiny teeth that are used to eat seaweed.

Long-spined sea urchins (*wana* in Hawaiian) wedge themselves into crevices on the reef and protect themselves with sharp, stinging spines.

The reef provides fishes with food, protection, and a place to have their young. Each kind of fish has its own special way of living on the reef.

The colorful butterflyfishes have very small mouths, but they are able to eat many things like tiny coral animals or other small animals that float in the water.

Many butterflyfishes have a black stripe that hides the eye and a false eye spot near the back of the body. These markings may confuse a predator about which end is the head and which is the tail.

This raccoon butterflyfish had a bite taken out of its tail, but it survived.

Surgeonfishes (sometimes called tangs) eat seaweed from the rocks. They have sharp spines near their tails that they use for protection.

The moorish idol with its bold design and long graceful upper fin is a beautiful sight. It eats sponges from crevices in the reef.

The reef triggerfish is often seen in Hawaiian waters. It has the long Hawaiian name *humuhumu-nukunuku-apua'a*. Triggerfishes slip into holes in the reef when threatened or when resting at night. They wedge themselves in tightly by raising a pointed spine above the eye.

Marjorie Awai

Wrasses feed on crabs, worms, and other small animals. They are a common sight on the reef.

Some sea animals help each other. Small yellow and purple cleaner wrasses pick tiny animals and dead scales off the bodies of other fishes.

The parrotfishes are larger relatives of the wrasses. They scrape small plants off the coral rock with their strong, sharp beak-like teeth. Coral, eaten along with the plants, is crushed into sand by another set of teeth in the throat. This sand is then eliminated, adding new sand to the reef. Male parrotfishes are bright green or blue; females are not as colorful.

Goatfishes use a pair of feelers on the chin (barbels) for searching in the sand and around rocks for small animals to eat.

Glenn Cummings

There are some long, skinny fishes on the reef. Trumpet-fish look like sticks floating in the water. They use their long mouths like a straw to suck up tiny animals.

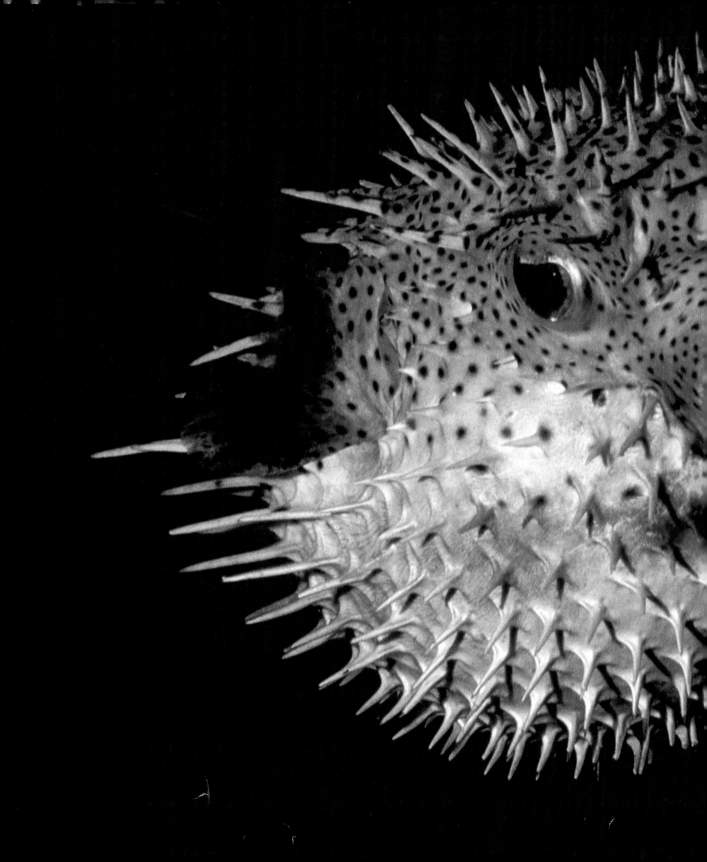

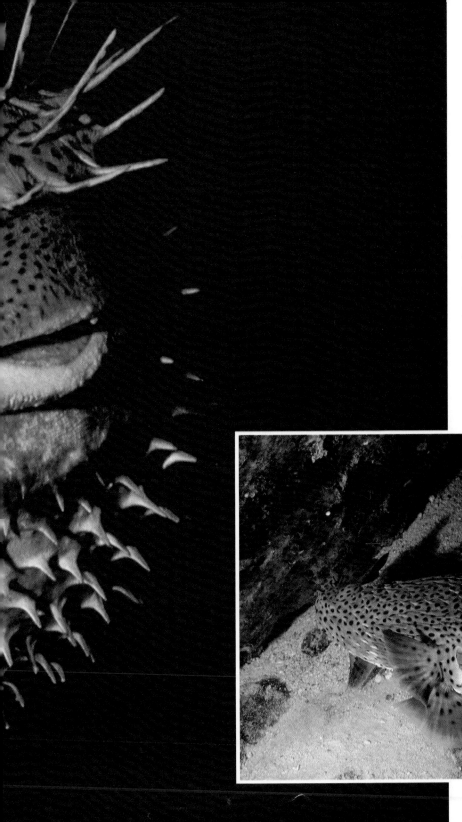

Some fishes have unusual ways to protect themselves. The pufferfish expands so it cannot be swallowed by most predators on the reef.

Other fishes hide themselves by looking like their surroundings (this is called camouflage). Predators like scorpionfishes, lizardfishes, anglerfishes, and flounders conceal themselves so that they cannot be seen by their prey.

Moray eels are long slithery fishes that move easily in and out of holes in the reef. Generally they hide during the day and come out at night to hunt for fish, crabs, and other small animals. They are usually not aggressive but their teeth are sharp and they defend their shelters. Keep your hands and fingers out of dark holes in the reef!

Lobsters live in caves and holes in the reef. Slipper lobsters have flat bodies that blend into the rocks.

An octopus has eight long arms with strong suction cups used for grasping things. It is hard to see because it looks very much like a rock. When threatened it can let out a cloud of black ink to conceal its escape.

You can see large sea animals that live in the ocean from a boat or in an aquarium.

Some fish protect themselves by swimming in a large group called a school. When a predator approaches it gets confused by the large, swirling mass of silvery bodies.

Sharks can move very quickly. They are powerful hunters that have strong teeth. Although they eat many kinds of marine animals they rarely attack people.

Whales are the largest animals living today. Like other mammals they breathe air. The young are born live and are nursed by their mothers. In the winter and early spring, humpback whales come to Hawaii to give birth to their young.

If you go whale watching you may see a whale slapping its tail or leaping out of the water (breaching). It makes a big splash when it lands!

Dolphins and porpoises are small whales. They sometimes swim and play near boats.

Sea turtles are reptiles, related to snakes and lizards. They swim deep in the ocean but need to come to the surface to breathe. They find their food on the reef. People have caught so many of them for meat, shells, and eggs that very few are left. Today there are laws against hunting sea turtles and collecting their eggs.

Hawaiian monk seals live on the small islands in the northwestern part of Hawaii, where there are no people. They are not found anywhere else in the world.

The life of the sea is like a beautiful pattern with many parts. Each animal and plant has its own way of living, but these are connected with the ways of living of all the other animals and plants. Enjoy the life of the ocean and protect all of its wonders.

Exploring Marine Life

Exploring Marine Life

Beach and Tidepools

You can have a wonderful time exploring the beach and tidepools. The best time to see the marine animals in these areas is at low tide (check the tide tables in the newspaper for the times).

The ocean is very powerful and should be approached with great care, especially when there are waves breaking on the shore. As waves vary in size and force, it is important never to turn your back on the ocean or go near the shore during periods of high surf. A wave can break unexpectedly, and large waves create dangerous currents. Children must be carefully supervised at the beach. When you explore the tidepools be sure to wear sneakers or reef tabis to keep from slipping or getting cut.

You will find marine life by observing carefully on the shore and in the water. You may turn over rocks to look underneath, but always put them back the way you found them; they are the animals'

homes. If an animal appears to be stuck to the rock don't force it off. Take animals out of the water for a short time only and touch them very gently. If you want to examine an animal more closely put it in a clear container filled with sea water while you look at it, then return it to the ocean.

Be careful to protect the marine environment. Put animals back where you found them. If you are collecting seaweed, don't pull it from the rock, instead pinch or clip it carefully, leaving some attached to the rock. Leave some shells so hermit crabs will be able to find new homes. Be sure to remove your trash and help keep the beach clean so that others can enjoy it too.

The Reef

Snorkeling is an easy and enjoyable way for adults and children to see marine life in shallow reef areas. All you need is a dive mask, snorkel, and fins. The mask allows you to see clearly in the water, the snorkel tube lets you breath while your face is in the water, and the fins make swimming easier. Snorkeling equipment comes in all sizes. It is important that yours fits properly.

Non-swimmers can lie on an air mattress or boogie board and look into the water through a mask. They should always be accompanied by a swimmer. A beginning snorkeler can float or swim gently at the surface enjoying the scene below. A child of five or six who knows how to swim can learn to snorkel. More experienced snorkelers can dive beneath the surface for a closer look.

A snorkeler swims by moving the fins slowly in a deep flutter kick. Hands and arms are used mostly for turning. Be careful not to splash the water and scare the fish!

The best snorkeling spots are over shallow reefs or near rocks. The calmer the water the more you can see; waves stir up the bottom making the water murky and creating currents. There are a number of snorkeling spots in Hawaii where the fish are somewhat tame and can be easily watched.

Hazardous Animals

Some marine animals are hazardous, so be careful to touch only those that you know are safe. Coral cuts and scrapes and puncture wounds like those caused by crabs and eels can become infected. Treat them as soon as possible by cleaning with fresh water and soap. Flood the area with peroxide and keep it dry, clean, and covered.

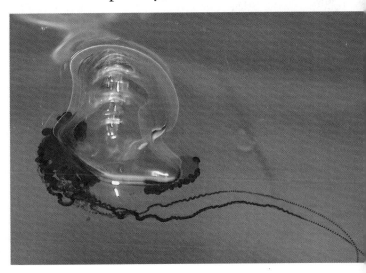

Long, thin-spined urchins *(wana)* can cause painful stings. Don't try to remove the small spines from the skin. Treat the irritation by soaking in hot water, dilute vinegar, or a solution of baking soda and water.

Portuguese-men-of-war, which look like small blue balloons, are common on Hawaii beaches after a storm. They have microscopic stingers in their tentacles that cause painful welts. Carefully remove the tentacles and do not rub the sting. Wash gently with alcohol and treat with unseasoned meat tenderizer for ten to fifteen minutes. These stings can be dangerous to persons allergic to the venom.

Stings from cone shells, scorpion fish, and sting rays contain venomous toxin. Hold cone shells by the broad end to avoid the stinger. Treat a sting by soaking in water as hot as you can stand for at least twenty minutes. If any injury produces severe symptoms, see a doctor.

Acknowledgments

We wish to express our very great appreciation to Ed Robinson, a talented underwater photographer, who provided the majority of the photographs that appear in this book. We are especially grateful for his willingness to make special trips to take new pictures for use here. Our thanks also to Marj Awai, Glenn Cummings, Doug Faulkner, and Colin Lau for providing additional photographs, and to Jeff Reese for the picture on the back cover.

Stephanie Feeney

We are very grateful to all of the children who appear in this book—especially Eric Diaz, Joshua Schacter, Kasumi Vitarelli, Brandon Riley, and John Bendon who cooperated patiently with our photographic demands. We appreciate the assistance of Lisa Diaz, Jeanne Riley, Kathy Oshiro, and Vicki Newbury for helping to set up the photo sessions. Special thanks to Charlene Doi and the staff of the Maui Pine Children's Center.

We are extremely grateful to Mary Morioka for her important contributions to the design and content of this book. Carol Hopper, Les Matsuura, and Ann Coopersmith provided invaluable consultation regarding marine life. We also wish to thank Sue Robinson, Eva Moravcik, and Diana and Jeremy Ginsburg for their contributions. Last, but by no means least, a very special thank you to Katie Aebi for the inspiration that led to the creation of this book and for its title.

The Authors

Stephanie Feeney, professor of education, is the early childhood education specialist at the University of Hawaii. She received degrees from UCLA, Harvard, and Claremont Graduate School. She is well known for writing, consulting, and lecturing on early childhood education. The author of an introductory textbook *Who Am I in the Lives of Children?*, she has written two previous children's books *A is for Aloha* and *Hawaii is a Rainbow*. She learned about the joys of the world beneath the sea from Ann Fielding.

Ann Fielding, a marine biologist, received her B.S. and M.S. degrees from the University of Hawaii. She was education specialist at the Waikiki Aquarium and research associate in the Department of Marine Biology at the Bishop Museum. She is author of *Hawaiian Reefs and Tidepools* and *An Underwater Guide to Hawai'i*. She currently lives on the island of Maui, where she teaches snorkeling, SCUBA diving, and marine biology, and she leads diving expeditions worldwide.

Stephanie Feeney, Ed Robinson, and Anne Fielding.

The Photographer

Ed Robinson, who took most of the photographs in this book, studied marine biology in California and then moved to Maui, where he has been diving and photographing the reef since 1971. His work appears in many publications including *National Geographic, Oceans Magazine, An Underwater Guide to Hawai'i, Hawaiian Reefs and Tidepools,* and *Maui on My Mind*.